Charles Wysocki's
Americana Cookbook

Charles Wysocki's
Americana
Cookbook

Text and recipes by Joni Miller

Harry N. Abrams, Inc., Publishers

Project Directors: Margaret L. Kaplan, Naomi Warner
Designer: Liz Trovato

Library of Congress Catalog Card Number: 94-73478
ISBN 0-8109-3978-9

Published in 1995 by Harry N. Abrams, Incorporated, New York
A Times Mirror Company

Printed and bound in Hong Kong

★ CONTENTS ★

Introduction

One flag, one land, one heart, one hand,
One Nation, evermore!

Oliver Wendell Holmes, Sr.

 For twenty-five years Charles Wysocki's memorable artistic vision of early American life has celebrated our nation's past in paintings that invite us to reflect on simpler times. Wysocki's world is the America where sentiment and patriotism coexisted with homely virtues and a nurturing family life. Where barn raisings and quilting bees brought folks together in honest industry followed by a friendly potluck supper. Where golden ears of corn and vine-ripened tomatoes sang of the seasons and enlivened a simple meal. Where marching bands wended their way down Main Streets everywhere and flags swayed in the breeze on the Fourth of July. Where courageous sea captains returned home from the sea bearing gifts of spices and silken shawls for loved ones and young sweethearts courted on hay rides. The enduring bounty of our land, harvested from coast to coast, sustained us then and sustains us now, a unique melting pot of good things to eat. It is these foods and those times that *Charles Wysocki's Americana Cookbook* honors.

6 1-inch-thick pork loin chops
All-purpose flour
Salt
Freshly ground black pepper
2 tablespoons vegetable oil
3 tablespoons unsalted butter
1 medium onion, minced
1 large tart apple, cored, pared, and
    thinly sliced
¾ cup ruby port
¾ cup homemade beef stock or
    canned beef broth
1 teaspoon orange zest
¼ teaspoon ground cinnamon
¼ teaspoon ground ginger
Pinch ground cloves
1 cup cranberries, sorted and rinsed in
    cold water
½ cup water
1 tablespoon sugar

Cape Cod Cranberry Pork Chops

Long before the Pilgrims landed in 1620, North American Indians prized the *sassamanesh,* a tart, round little red berry growing from low, trailing vines in the marshes of Massachusetts. Ground berries were an ingredient in pemmican and medicinal poultices, and their colorful juice was pressed into service as a dye for rugs and blankets. The cranberry very likely made an appearance at the first Thanksgiving, given a new name by the colonists who noticed its blossoms looked like the head of a crane.

Fresh cranberries are remarkably long-lasting and will stay fresh and flavorful for several months stored in the refrigerator in their original unopened plastic bag. They also freeze well; for a year-round supply, simply double-wrap the bags and store in the freezer for up to nine months.

Preheat oven to 325° F.

Trim the excess fat from the chops and pat dry with a paper towel. Combine the flour, salt, and pepper and dredge the chops with the mixture, shaking off any excess. In a medium-size heavy skillet, heat the vegetable oil and 2 tablespoons of the butter. Brown the chops 3 at a time for 1 minute on each side. Arrange the chops, overlapping slightly, in a shallow ovenproof casserole and set aside.

Pour off all but 2 tablespoons of fat from the skillet. Add the onion and sauté until golden, about 6 minutes. With a slotted spoon, remove the onion and set aside. Add the remaining tablespoon of butter and the sliced apple to the skillet and sauté over medium heat until golden, about 3 minutes. With a slotted spoon, remove the apple and set aside. Add the port, stock, orange zest, and all of the spices to the skillet. Bring to a boil, scraping up the brown bits from the bottom of the pan with a wooden spoon.

Pour the spiced wine mixture over the chops. Cover and cook for 25 minutes, turning once.

Meanwhile, in a small saucepan, combine the cranberries, water, and sugar, and bring to a boil over medium-high heat. Reduce the heat, simmer for 5 minutes, and drain.

Remove the casserole from the oven and spoon the reserved onion, apple, and cranberries over the chops. Return to the oven and cook for an additional 5 minutes, or until the chops are fork-tender.

Yield: 6 servings

Thrifty Turkey

2 to 3 cups well-seasoned bread
   stuffing
2 cups cooked turkey, diced
1 cup corn kernels
1 small red bell pepper, diced
6 scallions, chopped
1 cup milk
3 large eggs, beaten
2 tablespoons all-purpose flour
Salt and pepper to taste
¼ teaspoon Tabasco

 Wild turkey washed down with cider is said to have been part of the pilgrims' First Thanksgiving. Much later, Benjamin Franklin was such an admirer of the turkey that he lobbied to have it declared America's national emblem. These days, though turkey sales traditionally soar through the roof during the holidays, our national love of the bird has transformed it into a year-round favorite.

No matter the size of the bird or the group that gathers to savor it, somehow there's always leftover turkey waiting in the wings for an encore. Indeed, some folks believe the best part of Thanksgiving is when turkey is served the second time around. This savory "pie," which can be made any time of the year, tastes just like a miniature version of the whole holiday feast, especially if you serve it accompanied by cranberry relish.

Preheat oven to 400° F.

Lightly grease a 10-inch deep-dish pie plate or ovenproof casserole. Break apart the clumps of stuffing and evenly press them onto the bottom and sides of the pie plate to form a crust.

In a medium-size bowl, combine the turkey, corn, red bell pepper, and scallions. Set aside.

In a small bowl, combine the milk, eggs, flour, salt, pepper, and Tabasco. Beat lightly with a fork to combine, and pour over the turkey mixture. Stir gently.

Spoon the mixture into the stuffing "pie" shell and bake for 15 minutes. Lower the heat to 350° F. and cook another 30 to 35 minutes, or until golden on top.

Yield: 4 to 6 servings

> *Chowder breathes reassurance. It steams consolation.*
>
> Clementine Paddleford

New England Clam Chowder

¼ pound rindless salt pork, diced
2 medium onions, finely chopped
3 tablespoons all-purpose flour
2 large potatoes, peeled and diced
3 cups milk
2 cups bottled clam juice
2 cups fresh or frozen minced clams
Salt and freshly ground white pepper, to taste
1 cup heavy cream, light cream, or half and half
Chopped parsley, for garnish
3 tablespoons butter (optional)

Clam Chowder, New England's signature seafood dish, is said to derive its name from *chaudière*, the French word for cauldron. Although Native Americans introduced the colonists to clam digging and clambakes much earlier, it is likely that the delicious idea of combining milk with fish or shellfish was introduced to Massachusetts by settlers from the Channel Islands, who shared their culinary legacy along the state's shore in the 17th century. As is so often the case with America's great regional recipes, two areas claim to make the best, most authentic version. New Englanders literally see red when "the other chowder," milk-less, tomato-based Manhattan Clam Chowder, is mentioned.

This recipe saves a bit of time and effort by using the fresh or frozen minced clams available at many fish markets. Chowder tastes best if allowed to mellow in the refrigerator for a day. Serve with crackers and a green salad as a chilly-night main course.

In a heavy 4-quart saucepan over medium heat, sauté the salt pork until golden. Transfer it to a paper towel to drain. Pour off all but 2 tablespoons of the rendered fat.

Add the onions to the pan and cook, stirring, until soft and translucent but not browned. Sprinkle the flour over the onion and cook, stirring constantly, for 2 to 3 minutes. Add the potatoes, the milk, and the clam juice. Bring to a simmer, cover, and cook until the potatoes are tender, about 10 to 15 minutes (do not allow the liquid to boil). Add the minced clams, salt and pepper, and cream. Bring to a simmer and cook for 5 minutes.

Remove pan from the heat and let the chowder stand at room temperature for 1 hour to improve its texture.

Reheat and garnish with the crisped bits of salt pork, a sprinkling of chopped parsley, and a bit of butter.

Yield: 4 to 6 servings

For the wings:
4 pounds chicken wings (about 20 to 24 wings)
Peanut or vegetable oil for deep frying
5 tablespoons unsalted butter
1 tablespoon white wine vinegar
2 to 3 tablespoons Louisiana-style hot sauce such as Tabasco or Crystal
1 teaspoon paprika

For the blue cheese dressing:
½ cup mayonnaise
½ cup regular or low-fat sour cream
½ cup regular or low-fat plain yogurt
1 clove garlic, minced
1 tablespoon white wine vinegar
1 tablespoon fresh lemon juice
½ cup crumbled blue cheese
Salt and freshly ground black pepper, to taste

Buffalo-Style Chicken Wings

with

Blue Cheese Dressing

Some American food traditions are newer than others. Take Buffalo-Style Chicken Wings, for example. It's been only a little over twenty years since the late Teressa Bellissimo of Frank and Teressa's Anchor Bar and Restaurant in Buffalo, New York, whipped up the first batch of this popular Northeastern snack that has literally spread its wings across America. One night after the kitchen had closed, Mrs. Bellissimo's son and his friends asked for something to eat. About to make stock from chicken wings, the quick-thinking mother improvised a recipe with memorable results.

The piping hot spicy wings are always served along with crisp, chilled celery stalks and carrot sticks and a soothing, creamy blue cheese dressing.

Rinse the wings and pat dry with a paper towel. Cut off the wing tips (save them to use for soup later). Halve the wings at the joint. Trim excess fat.

Pour 1 to 1½ inches of oil into a deep-fryer or large saucepan. Heat the oil to 370° F. Adding as many wings as will fit in a single layer, fry the wings in batches, turning once, until golden brown and cooked through, about 8 to 10 minutes. Drain on paper towels. Place the wings in a large bowl and set aside.

In a small saucepan over low heat, melt the butter. Stir in the vinegar, hot sauce, and paprika. Pour the sauce over the wings and toss until evenly coated.

In a medium-size bowl, mix together all of the ingredients except the blue cheese. Gently fold in the blue cheese (the dressing will be lumpy). Season to taste with salt and pepper. Cover and chill. Serve cold.

Yield: 6 servings

*And this is good old Boston,
The home of the bean
and the cod…*

John Collins Bossidy

*1 pound dried Great Northern or navy
(Yankee) beans (approx. 2 cups),
rinsed and picked over*
*1 small onion stuck with 3 whole
cloves*
¼ pound salt pork with rind
1 medium onion, chopped
*3 tablespoons firmly packed brown
sugar*
¼ cup dark unsulphured molasses
2 teaspoons English-style dry mustard
¼ teaspoon ground ginger
Freshly ground black pepper
1 bay leaf, optional
1 teaspoon salt

Bean Town's Best Baked Beans

When necessity is the mother of invention, great regional American dishes like this one are often the result. In 17th-century Massachusetts, the Puritan sabbath began at sundown on Saturday and ended Sunday night. During this period no work of any kind was allowed. But families still had to eat, so first thing Saturday morning resourceful Puritan homemakers set a pot of beans to simmer in the fireplace. By Saturday night the slowly cooked beans, nourishing and redolent of molasses and onions, were ready for supper. Leftover beans reappeared the following morning at breakfast, served along with codfish cakes and Boston brown bread. This cooking custom is how Boston came to be nicknamed "Bean Town."

For a hearty Bean Town Saturday supper, serve accompanied by Boston brown bread, coleslaw, applesauce, and pickles.

In a colander, rinse and sort the beans, removing tiny pebbles or dirt. Put the beans in a large bowl, cover completely with water, and soak from 6 to 12 hours. Overnight is best, since a longer soaking time allows gas-causing elements to dissolve.

Drain and rinse the beans. Place in a large saucepan. Add the clove-studded onion and enough water to cover the beans by about 2 inches. Bring to a boil over medium-high heat, skim off the white foam, reduce heat to low, and simmer, partially covered, until the beans are tender but still firm, about 30 minutes. Remove and discard the onion. Drain the beans and transfer to a 2½ quart Dutch oven or beanpot.

Preheat oven to 250° F.

Blanch the salt pork in simmering water for 3 minutes. Drain. Score the fat side in a ½-inch diamond pattern without cutting into the rind. Set aside.

In a medium-size bowl, combine the chopped onion, brown sugar, molasses, mustard, ginger, and pepper with 2 cups of water and stir well. Pour the mixture over the beans, add the bay leaf, and stir. Add enough water to cover the beans. Press the salt pork rind side down on top of the beans. Cover tightly, and bake for about 3½ to 4 hours, adding water as needed. Remove cover from beans, stir in the salt, and add a small amount of water if beans seem dry. Bake uncovered for 30 minutes, or until the top forms a caramel-brown crust and the interior is almost dry and syrupy. Discard the bay leaf before serving.

Yield: 6 servings

Progress in civilization has been accompanied by progress in cookery.

Fannie Farmer

Pilgrim's Pleasure Sausage, Chestnut, and Apple Stuffing

½ cup chopped onion

1 tablespoon unsalted butter

½ pound pork sausage

2 medium-sized Granny Smith apples (approx. ½ pound), peeled, cored, and chopped, to make 2 cups

½ cup chopped, peeled, roasted chestnuts (pecans or walnuts may be substituted)

1 tablespoon dried sage or 1 teaspoon fresh sage

1 teaspoon dried thyme

1 teaspoon dried marjoram

2 large eggs, beaten

4 cups ½-inch bread cubes (6 thick slices of firm-textured white bread)

According to John Mariani, author of *The Dictionary of American Food and Drink* (Hearst Books), the word stuffing comes from the verb "to stuff" and the term first appeared in print in English in 1538 to describe fillings made of meats, vegetables, grains, and other ingredients that were added to meat, poultry, and fish. During the Victorian era in America, a period when propriety counted above all else, polite society began referring to it as dressing. Both terms are used today; if you live in the East or the South, you're more likely to still be calling it stuffing. Since we tend to stuff ourselves at the Thanksgiving table it makes sense that the turkey, too, would be stuffed.

Stuffing, or dressing, should star at more than the Thanksgiving table. Its versatility dresses up all kinds of main dishes, so this recipe really shouldn't be limited to holiday use.

Preheat oven to 325° F.

Grease 8 6-ounce ramekins or custard cups.

In a small skillet, sauté the onion in the butter until soft, but not browned.

In a large bowl combine the sausage, onion, apples, chestnuts, sage, and eggs. Mix together well. Add the bread cubes and gently stir until blended.

Spoon the stuffing into the ramekins, gently pressing the stuffing into shape. Cover each ramekin with foil and set on a baking sheet. Bake for 30 minutes. Remove the foil covers and bake another 10 minutes, until the stuffing is hot and lightly browned on top.

To unmold, run a knife around the edge of each ramekin and unmold onto a platter.

Yield: 8 servings

Star-Spangled Strawberry Shortcake

4 pints strawberries, rinsed and hulled
1/4 cup sugar
2 cups all-purpose flour
1 tablespoon baking powder
3 tablespoons sugar
Dash of salt
1/2 cup chilled, unsalted butter, cut into pieces
3/4 cup heavy cream
Melted butter for tops of biscuits (optional)

For the topping:
1 cup heavy cream, whipped to moist peaks

 What's synonymous with summer, Fourth of July feasts, and picnics under the shade of a tree? The luscious all-American strawberry shortcake, second only to Mom's apple pie as this nation's most delectable dessert. The sweetened baking powder biscuits, crumbly inside, crisp on the outside, take their name from being made "short" with butter.

Our plenitude of strawberry patches spawned a period of "strawberry fever" during the 1850s, which found horticultural societies holding strawberry exhibitions and towns throwing strawberry festivals where the berry was celebrated in treats like strawberry fritters, pies, shortcakes, and ice cream. All-strawberry parties and dinners became the rage, and shortcakes cut into ladylike triangles appeared on silver trays at elegant afternoon tea parties.

This recipe makes enough shortcakes to serve family and friends. Leftover biscuits are good for breakfast the next morning.

Cut the strawberries in half lengthwise and toss with the 1/4 cup of sugar. Cover and set aside to mellow for 1/2 to 1 hour. Stir occasionally.

Preheat oven to 400° F.

In a medium-size mixing bowl, sift together the flour, baking powder, 3 tablespoons of sugar, and salt. Using your fingertips or a pastry blender, cut the butter pieces into the flour mixture until it resembles coarse meal. Pour in half the cream and stir with a fork. Add the remaining cream, a bit at a time, until the dry ingredients are moist and the dough comes away clean from the sides of the bowl. (You may not need all the cream.)

Gather the dough together in a ball and turn it out on a lightly floured work surface. Lightly flour your hands and knead the dough gently and quickly about 8 times, or until it feels soft and firm, but not sticky.

Using a rolling pin in light, swift strokes, roll the dough into a 1/2-inch thick circle. Cut out the biscuits with a 3-inch floured cutter, taking care not to twist the cutter. Gather together leftover dough, knead briefly, roll out again, and cut out the rest of the biscuits. If desired, brush tops with melted butter.

Place on an ungreased baking sheet. Bake for 10 to 15 minutes, or until the tops are lightly golden. Remove from oven and cool briefly.

While still warm, split the shortcakes apart. Spoon some of the strawberries and their juice over the bottom of each biscuit. Add a dollop of whipped cream and top with the other half of the biscuit. Decorate with more whipped cream.

Yield: 10 shortcakes

Eternity is a ham and two people.

Dorothy Parker

8 to 10 pound cooked ham
2 tablespoons prepared mustard
1 cup brown sugar
½ cup honey

Company's Coming Honey-Mustard Glazed Ham

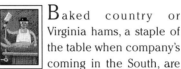

Baked country or Virginia hams, a staple of the table when company's coming in the South, are traditionally decorated by removing the skin from the fully cooked ham and scoring the fat in diagonal slashes with a sharp knife to make a pretty diamond pattern. For further adornment and a bit of extra flavor, a whole clove is stuck into the center of each diamond. Such hams, which are saltier than the fully cooked tenderized smoked hams sold in most supermarkets, can be glazed with any number of mixtures, from simple brown sugar and bread crumbs to elaborately spiced versions that call for the luxurious inclusion of Champagne. This Honey-Mustard Glaze is sweet, with a bit of punch from the mustard. If you want to add more visual flair than whole cloves offer, garnish the ham with pineapple rings after it is glazed and secure each ring with a toothpick speared through a maraschino cherry.

Preheat oven to 300° F.

In a small bowl, combine the mustard, brown sugar, and honey. Mix well.

Spread the mixture over the cooked ham and garnish as desired.

Put the ham back in the same pan it was baked in and heat it for 30 minutes. Remove from the pan and serve on your prettiest platter.

1 pound skinless, boneless chicken
    thighs (about 4 large), or 2 whole
    skinless, boneless chicken breasts
    (about 8 ounces each)
2 tablespoons flour
½ teaspoon salt
½ teaspoon ground red (cayenne)
    pepper
Freshly ground black pepper
2 tablespoons olive oil or unsalted butter
1 medium onion, thinly sliced
1 small green bell pepper, seeded and
    cut into thin strips
1 small red bell pepper, seeded and cut
    into thin strips
2 large cloves garlic, chopped
2 teaspoons curry powder
¾ teaspoon dried thyme leaves,
    crumbled
1 14½-ounce can whole tomatoes,
    with liquid
¼ cup dried currants
½ cup sliced almonds, toasted

Country Captain

This cozy chicken dish, tasty any time of the year, is easy and exotic. The secret to its unique flavor is curry powder, a spice mixture more closely associated with India than America, and therein lies a roundabout culinary tale. Some historians believe a British colonial army officer brought this unusual chicken recipe home to England after serving in India, where local soldiers were called "country troops" and their native leaders were known as "country captains." Others speculate it was named for early American sea captains who returned to their homes along the coast of Georgia bearing gifts of rare and unusual spices for their wives.

You'll want to look for the best quality imported curry powder available at the supermarket or specialty food store. Curry powder blends vary, but most include coriander, cumin, turmeric, fenugreek, celery seed, and fennel.

Trim fat from the chicken if necessary. Rinse the pieces and pat dry with a paper towel. In a shallow bowl, combine the flour, salt, cayenne, and black pepper. Toss the chicken with the seasoned flour.

Heat the olive oil or butter in a large, heavy skillet over medium-high heat. Add the chicken and sauté about 3 minutes per side, or until it is light brown and opaque (it will not be completely cooked). Remove the chicken from the skillet. Set aside. Reduce heat to medium.

Using the same skillet, add the onion and bell peppers, and sauté for 4 to 5 minutes, or until the vegetables soften. Add the garlic, curry powder, and thyme and cook, stirring constantly, for 1 minute. Add the tomatoes with their liquid. Break the tomatoes up with a spoon. Reduce heat to medium-low, cover, and simmer for 15 minutes. Uncover, stir in the currants, and cook 5 minutes, or until the chicken is tender.

Garnish with toasted almonds and serve over steaming mounds of hot rice.

Yield: 4 to 6 servings

Maryland Crab Cakes

1 pound fresh lump or backfin
   crabmeat, picked over
1 large egg
2 tablespoons mayonnaise
1 teaspoon Worcestershire sauce
1/2 teaspoon dry mustard, or
   1 teaspoon Dijon mustard
1 teaspoon Old Bay seasoning
1/4 teaspoon freshly ground black
   pepper
Dash of Tabasco sauce
3 tablespoons chopped fresh parsley,
   optional
1/2 cup finely crushed cracker crumbs
2 tablespoons peanut oil
2 tablespoons unsalted butter

 What gumbo is to New Orleans and chili is to Texas, crab cakes are to Maryland. Every cook in the Chesapeake Bay claims to have the one and only recipe for these succulent patties that make the most of the region's succulent blue crabs, whose name comes from the blue underside of their claws. One of the most famous versions was a specialty of the Baltimore & Ohio Railroad, the line that pioneered dining on the rails by serving the first meal aboard a train in one of its "refectory cars" in 1842. The cakes should be served hot from the skillet, accompanied by tartar sauce, French fries, and coleslaw or potato salad.

Lump crabmeat is large white chunks from the body; less expensive backfin, also white, is sold in smaller chunks. Dark claw meat can also be used but won't be as tasty. Old Bay seasoning can be found in the spice section of most large supermarkets across the country.

Place the crabmeat in a medium-size bowl. Set aside.

In a small bowl, combine the egg, mayonnaise, Worcestershire sauce, mustard, Old Bay seasoning, black pepper, Tabasco sauce, and parsley. Whisk together until frothy.

Sprinkle the cracker crumbs over the crabmeat. Pour in the seasoned egg mixture. With your hands, gently fold the ingredients together. Be careful not to break up the chunks of crabmeat.

Gently shape the crabmeat mixture into slightly rounded 1-inch-thick cakes about 3 inches in diameter. Avoid pressing too firmly; the cakes should just hold together. Cover and refrigerate for 1 hour.

Heat the peanut oil and butter together in a large skillet over medium-high heat. Fry the cakes about 3 minutes on each side, or until golden brown.

Drain on paper towels and serve piping hot.

Yield: 4 to 6 servings

2 cups water
1 cup milk
1 teaspoon salt
2 tablespoons unsalted butter
1 cup stone-ground cornmeal
3 large eggs, separated

Dixie Spoonbread

Without a doubt spoonbread is one of the most elegant dishes in the repertoire of traditional Southern cuisine. Despite its name, spoonbread is really a country cousin of the French soufflé, with a close kinship to custard and pudding. Moist and light, with a creamy texture and lush corn flavor, it puffs up to form a lovely golden brown crown as it bakes. Most likely its name came from the big spoon used to serve it up piping hot from the baking dish. The few ingredients are nothing out of the ordinary, but a magical transformation occurs when cornmeal is infused with scalded milk, allowing the true essence of corn flavor to spring vividly to life. To create a zippy Southwestern version, add one 4-ounce can of mild green chiles, drained and minced, before baking.

As a suppertime side dish it goes nicely alongside everything from stew and roasted chicken to baked ham and sautéed vegetables. Thomas Jefferson liked to eat leftover spoonbread for breakfast at his Monticello home. To follow his example, simply chill, slice, and brown in a skillet with a bit of butter.

Preheat oven to 400° F.

In a medium-size saucepan over medium-high heat, bring the water, milk, and salt to a boil. Reduce the heat to low, and slowly add the cornmeal, stirring constantly. Simmer, stirring frequently, for 2 to 3 minutes, or until the mixture thickens.

Remove the pan from the heat and stir in the egg yolks.

In a separate bowl, beat the egg whites until stiff, but not dry, peaks form. Gently fold the beaten whites into the cornmeal and yolk mixture.

Spoon the mixture into a greased 2-quart soufflé dish or casserole. Place the dish on a baking sheet and bake for 30 minutes, or until puffed and golden brown. Serve hot.

Yield: 6 to 8 servings

1 cup dried black-eyed peas
1 clove garlic, finely chopped
¾ cup chopped celery
¾ cup chopped onion
⅓ cup chopped green pepper
¾ pound smoked ham, chopped
½ teaspoon dried thyme
¼ teaspoon dried sage
2 tablespoons white wine vinegar
3 tablespoons olive oil
¼ cup chopped parsley
1 medium tomato, peeled, seeded, and
    finely chopped
1 cup white rice
Tabasco sauce to taste
Chopped scallions for garnish

Hoppin' John

Good luck comes to those who eat black-eyed peas, a staple of the Southern larder that's believed to possess mystical powers. It's said that eating black-eyed peas on New Year's day will ensure good luck for an entire year. And if you serve a bowl of collard greens alongside, symbolizing "folding" money, financial prosperity will also come your way. One theory is that the peas signify plenty of pocket change, while another school of thought suggests that you'll have as much money as the number of peas you eat. Hoppin' John's colorful name probably originated during the plantation era, named for a lame cook who hopped up and down while stirring the pot on the stove.

This version calls for dried black-eyed peas, but if you're short of time, frozen ones straight from the unthawed package may be substituted. Serve as a hearty main dish accompanied by greens and corn bread, or as a side dish with pork, ham, or roasted chicken. Leftover Hoppin' John can be tossed with mixed greens for a tasty quick salad.

Rinse and sort the black-eyed peas, removing any stones or grit. Soak in water overnight. Drain well.

Combine the soaked, drained peas, garlic, celery, onion, green pepper, ham, thyme, and sage in a medium-size nonreactive saucepan. Add water to cover, bring to a boil and simmer, covered, for 35 to 40 minutes, or until the peas are tender but not too soft.

While the peas are simmering, combine the vinegar, olive oil, and parsley in a small bowl. When the peas are tender, drain them and reserve the cooking liquid. Add the oil and vinegar mixture and tomato to the peas in the saucepan.

In another saucepan, combine the reserved cooking liquid with enough water to measure 2 cups. Add the rice, bring to a boil and cook, covered, over low heat for 18 to 20 minutes, or until the rice is done. Add the peas to the rice and heat just long enough to warm the peas through. Season to taste with Tabasco sauce and garnish with chopped scallions.

Yield: 6 servings

> A world without tomatoes is like a string quartet without violins.
>
> Laurie Colwin in *Home Cooking*

Sarah Fritschner's Savory Tomato Cobbler

The tomato filling:
4 tablespoons unsalted butter
1/4 cup chopped onion
1 rib celery, minced
2 pounds fresh tomatoes (about 6 medium tomatoes)
1 teaspoon sugar
1/4 teaspoon salt
Freshly ground black pepper, to taste

The biscuit topping:
1/2 cup stoneground cornmeal
1 1/2 cups unbleached, all-purpose flour
2 1/2 teaspoons baking powder
1/2 teaspoon baking soda
1/2 teaspoon salt
3 tablespoons cold, unsalted butter
3 tablespoons chilled vegetable shortening
3/4 cup buttermilk

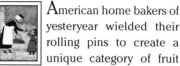 American home bakers of yesteryear wielded their rolling pins to create a unique category of fruit desserts whose whimsical names make us smile today. Pandowdies, betties, slumps, grunts, and cobblers each combined pie or biscuit dough with a sweetened fruit filling. This unusual non-dessert cobbler made with vine-ripened tomatoes and onions is a twist on tradition, producing an utterly delightful savory side dish that is a perfect accompaniment to baked ham. As a main dish served with a big green salad, it makes a perfect, light summer supper. It is believed cobblers were named for their toppings' resemblance to cobblestones. A hint of cornmeal in this dough gives the biscuits a "freckled" brown surface and adds an extra touch of flavor. For a variation, use crisp, slightly sweet and mildly flavored Vidalia onions from Georgia (available during a short harvest season from mid-May through July).

Preheat oven to 400° F.

Melt the butter in a large skillet over medium heat. Add the onion and celery and cook until the celery is tender.

Peel the tomatoes by dipping them into boiling water for 15 seconds. Drain, peel, and core the tomatoes and cut them into quarters (or eighths if they are very large). Stir the tomatoes into the onion-celery mixture along with the sugar, salt, and pepper. Spoon into an 8-inch-square ovenproof casserole.

To make the biscuit topping, combine the cornmeal, flour, baking powder, baking soda, and salt in a food processor. Whirl briefly to blend. Cut the butter and shortening into small pieces, add to the processor bowl, and process with quick on and off pulses until the largest bits are the size of small peas. Transfer to a large mixing bowl and add the buttermilk, stirring until the mixture holds together. Knead the dough briefly on a lightly floured board until it is smooth. Roll out to 1/2-inch thickness and cut into 2-inch rounds with a cookie cutter. Arrange the biscuits on top of the tomatoes.

Bake for 20 minutes, or until the biscuit topping is lightly browned.

Yield: 6 to 8 servings

33

1 cup corn oil
*4 large eggs, room temperature,
        lightly beaten*
⅔ cup water
2 cups canned pumpkin purée
3⅓ cups sifted all-purpose flour
1½ teaspoons salt
1 teaspoon ground nutmeg
1 teaspoon ground cinnamon
2 teaspoons baking soda
3 cups granulated sugar
½ cup golden raisins
*½ cup coarsely chopped walnuts
        or pecans*

Pumpkin Patch Tea Bread

Come autumn, the fields, farmers' markets, and supermarkets spring to life with mountains of pumpkins just waiting to be turned into pies, muffins, breads, and harvest-time soups. Our national passion for the pumpkin originated with Native Americans who in all probability brought a few along to the first Thanksgiving feast, where they would have been baked whole in the embers of a dying fire. For the flavor of fall year-round, turn to the contemporary pumpkin patch — canned pumpkin purée. Unlike most canned or frozen ingredients, this is nearly as good as homemade as long as you avoid the presweetened and spiced versions labeled "pumpkin pie filling."

These homey loaves will develop a richer, more mellow flavor if allowed to age for several days. For a perfect teatime treat, serve thinly sliced with cream cheese whipped with a little honey and dotted with a few bits of chopped crystallized ginger. The recipe makes enough for sharing with your neighbors.

Preheat oven to 350° F.
Grease and flour three 9 x 5 x 3-inch loaf pans.

In a large mixing bowl, combine the corn oil, eggs, water, and pumpkin purée. Sift together the flour, salt, nutmeg, cinnamon, and baking soda. Stir the dry ingredients into the pumpkin mixture. Add the sugar and mix thoroughly. Stir in the raisins and walnuts.

Spoon the batter into the prepared pans, gently pushing the mixture into the corners.

Bake for one hour, or until a metal skewer inserted in the center comes out clean and dry.

Remove the breads from the oven and allow to cool for 10 minutes before turning out of the pans. Will stay moist for 8 to 10 days tightly wrapped in foil or plastic wrap. Need not be refrigerated.

Yield: 3 loaves

EAT Laugh and Enjoy The Earth
and feed your Love for all it's Worth.

© Charles Wysocki

In the childhood memories of every good cook, there's a large kitchen, a warm stove, a simmering pot and a mom.

Barbara Costikyan

Mom's Pot Roast

The pleasures of pot roast cut across every region of America. For wherever there's a thrifty, skilled home cook, there's bound to be a succulent, comforting pot roast on the table surrounded by a nest of tender vegetables with gravy so good you can scarcely believe your taste-buds. Changing attitudes about what we eat have practically made pot roast an endangered species, but it's worth remembering that from time to time, when you yearn for the favorite flavors of childhood, nothing beats the nurturing goodness of this choice dish that makes the most of less expensive cuts of meat.

3- to 4-pound bottom round roast,
   tied to hold its shape
1/2 cup flour
Salt and pepper, to taste
2 tablespoons vegetable oil
2 cups homemade beef stock or
   canned beef broth
1/2 cup red wine
2 cloves garlic, crushed
1 bay leaf
1 teaspoon dried thyme
1/2 teaspoon salt
1/2 teaspoon freshly ground
   black pepper
1 small onion stuck with 3 or
   4 whole cloves
8 medium-size carrots, cut into
   3-inch pieces
6 medium-size boiling potatoes, peeled
   and quartered
3 medium-size turnips, peeled and
   quartered
1/2 cup water

Blot the moisture from the meat with a paper towel. Combine the flour, salt, and pepper and dredge the meat with it, tapping off any excess. Reserve the remaining flour.

In a 5-quart Dutch oven over medium-high heat, heat the oil. Put the roast in the pot and brown it thoroughly, turning to ensure that all sides brown, about 20 minutes. If there is more than 1/2 inch of oil remaining, drain some of it off.

Add the beef stock, red wine, garlic, bay leaf, thyme, salt, and pepper and reduce heat to low. Cover and simmer for 2 hours, turning the roast occasionally.

Add the onion, carrots, potatoes, and turnips, and simmer, covered, until the meat and vegetables are tender, about 30 to 45 minutes. The meat juices should run clear when pierced with a fork; the vegetables should be fork-tender.

Remove the meat and vegetables from the pan, place on a warmed platter. Remove the string. Cover the platter loosely with a piece of foil and let rest 30 minutes.

Discard the bay leaf and skim the fat from the juices in the pan. Over medium heat, bring the pan juices to a simmer. In a small bowl, whisk together the reserved dredging flour (about 1/2 cup) and the 1/2 cup water. Stir the mixture, a little at a time, into the simmering pan juices and cook until the gravy thickens, about 2 minutes.

Slice the pot roast against the grain and serve with the vegetables and gravy.

Yield: 6 servings

4 1-pound 14-ounce jars of
    commercial dill pickles,
    without garlic or garlic oil
3 cups granulated sugar
3 cups apple cider vinegar
2 cups water
1 6½-ounce jar pimientos, diced

Mrs. Ann Bosveld's Midwestern Made-over Refrigerator Dill Pickles

Pantry shelves lined with gleaming jars of home-made pickles, relishes, jams, and jellies have been a source of pride for generations of American home cooks. Inventor John L. Mason, a farm boy from New Jersey, paved the way to "putting up" peak-of-perfection fruits and vegetables in 1858 when he patented a revolutionary improved screw-capped glass jar.

This recipe from Iowa has occupied a place of honor in the family recipe file for three generations. Convenient and easy, it combines the best of the old and the new, allowing modern cooks to gussy up store-bought pickles with old-fashioned flavor. Crisp and slightly sweet with a hint of tanginess, these pickles will add just the right caring touch to a potluck supper or weekend picnic.

Remove the pickles from the jars and drain well. Cut the pickles into irregular 1-inch chunks and place in a large heat-proof mixing bowl. Add the pimientos, stir, and set aside.

In a large non-reactive saucepan over medium-high heat, combine the sugar, vinegar, and water and bring to a boil, stirring with a wooden spoon to dissolve the sugar. Remove from heat and pour the hot liquid over the pickles and pimientos. Stir well to coat the pickles with the brine and evenly distribute the pimiento.

Pack in hot, sterile canning jars. Let stand undisturbed in the refrigerator overnight to allow the flavors to blend. The pickles should be kept refrigerated; they will keep for up to two months.

To sterilize jars: Wash in hot, soapy water, then rinse in scalding water. Fill a large kettle with the jars, lids, and rubber rings. Cover with hot water. Bring the water to a boil and boil for 5 minutes. Turn off the heat and allow the containers to stand in the water. About 10 minutes before you are ready to fill the jars, place them along with the lids and rings on a rack to dry. They should still be hot when they are filled.

The Best Buttermilk Biscuits

Take two biscuits and pass them while they're hot.

Anonymous

2 cups all-purpose flour
2½ teaspoons baking powder
½ teaspoon baking soda
½ teaspoon salt
5 tablespoons chilled vegetable shortening
¾ cup buttermilk

For generations, plates of piping hot biscuits graced the American table at nearly every meal. According to folk wisdom, you had to have a tender heart to bake a tender biscuit, a quality that was sometimes referred to as "a touch of grace." A light touch combining and rolling out the ingredients helps, too.

Our grandmothers knew that rerolling leftover dough toughens it. So they thriftily turned the scraps into treats for the children by gently rolling bits of dough between their palms, forming two- or three-inch-long logs and setting them to bake alongside the "perfect" biscuits. In some families these crusty morsels were called "puppy-dog tails" or "bits and pieces."

Preheat oven to 450° F.

In a large bowl, sift together the flour, baking powder, baking soda, and salt. Cut the vegetable shortening into very small pieces. Using your fingertips or a pastry blender, cut the shortening pieces into the flour mixture until it resembles coarse meal.

Pour in the buttermilk and stir quickly with a fork until the dry ingredients are moistened and the dough comes away clean from the sides of the bowl.

Gently gather the dough into a ball and turn it out onto a lightly floured work board. Lightly dust the top of the dough with flour. Flour your hands and knead the dough gently and quickly about 8 times, or until it feels soft and firm, but not sticky.

Using a rolling pin in light, swift strokes, roll the dough into a ½-inch thick circle. Cut out the biscuits with a 2-inch floured cutter, taking care not to twist the cutter.

Place on an ungreased baking sheet. For soft biscuits, place the rounds close together with their sides nearly touching; for crisp ones, place the rounds 1-inch apart. Bake for 15 to 20 minutes, or until the tops are golden-brown. Serve piping hot.

Yield: 10 to 12 biscuits

2 cups granulated sugar
4 cups cold water
3 cups freshly squeezed lemon juice
   (about 12 large lemons)
6 cups cold water, sparkling water,
   or seltzer
Lemon and fresh mint for garnish

Front Porch Lemonade

Back before air conditioners and commercial soft drinks, the best defense against the relentless summer sun was a tall, frosty glass of lemonade sipped in leisurely fashion on the front porch rocker. Made with fresh spring water and cooled with shavings from the big block of ice kept wrapped in straw and sawdust in the ice house or cellar, it sat in a stoneware crock, ready to refresh when the temperature soared.

Then, as now, almost all of the lemons came from Southern California, where Franciscan friars established some of the first lemon groves in the late 1770s.

Though you'd never guess it, lemonade has a political past. It played a role in the temperance movement, where it was promoted as a healthful alternative to alcohol. Temperance crusader Lucy Hayes, the militant teetotaler wife of President Rutherford B. Hayes, was nicknamed "Lemonade Lucy" by her enemies.

When buying lemons, heft them in the palm of your hand and choose ones that are heaviest in proportion to their size. Before squeezing, roll them across the countertop with your hand and they will yield more juice.

In a medium-size saucepan, combine the sugar and cold water. Bring to a boil over high heat, stirring with a wooden spoon. Continue to boil for about 5 minutes, or until the mixture turns clear. Set aside to cool. (Refrigerated syrup will keep for a month.)

In a large pitcher, combine the lemon juice and syrup with the water, sparkling water, or seltzer. Stir and pour into tall ice-filled glasses. Garnish with a thin slice of lemon and a sprig of fresh mint.

For a contemporary pink lemonade, add a splash of cranberry juice.

Yield: 6 to 8 glasses

4 flour tortillas
1 tablespoon butter
1 tablespoon vegetable oil
½ small onion, diced
1 4-ounce can diced green chiles, drained
2 cups diced cooked potatoes
Salt and pepper, to taste
4 large eggs
2 teaspoons water
2 dashes Tabasco sauce
1 cup (4 ounces) shredded Monterey Jack cheese with jalapeños
⅓ cup commercial salsa
¼ cup chopped cilantro

Cross-cultural Breakfast Burritos

The melting pot that is American cuisine never ceases to make new connections, absorbing and adapting new and unusual flavors to create a cross-cultural repertoire of innovative dishes uniquely suited to the American way of life. When the flavors of the Southwest merged with our need for fast nourishment at breakfast time, the result was these unusual burritos. Serve them for breakfast, brunch, lunch, or a light supper. For variety, add bits of sautéed breakfast sausage, sizzled ham, or a few strips of bacon.

Preheat oven to 325° F.

Fold the tortillas in half, wrap in foil and place in the preheated oven to warm for 5 minutes.

In a 10-inch skillet over medium heat, combine the butter and vegetable oil, and heat until just melted. Add the onion and cook until softened, but not crisp, about 4 minutes.

Add the green chiles and potatoes to the skillet and cook until the potatoes are browned and crispy. Season with salt and pepper to taste.

In a small bowl, lightly beat the eggs with the water and Tabasco sauce and pour the mixture into the skillet. Cook, stirring occasionally, until the eggs are just set but still creamy. Remove the skillet from the heat and stir in half of the cheese.

Remove the tortillas from the oven and set one on each plate. Divide the egg mixture evenly among the tortillas. Top each burrito with a spoonful of salsa, and sprinkle with the cilantro and cheese.

Fold opposite sides of each filled tortilla over the topping about two inches. Fold one of the other sides of the tortilla halfway across the filling and roll the burrito into a plump "log."

Serve with a little dish of extra salsa on the side.

Yield: 4 servings

Wish I had time for just one more bowl of chili.

Kit Carson's last words

3 tablespoons vegetable oil
4 pounds lean beef chuck,
  cut into 1/2-inch pieces
1 large onion, finely chopped
3 garlic cloves, minced
1 teaspoon ground cumin
1 teaspoon dried oregano
3 tablespoons chili powder,
  or more to taste
1 28-ounce can Italian plum tomatoes,
  chopped
1 cup green chiles, chopped
1 teaspoon salt
2 cups water

Chuckwagon Chili

Will Rogers called it the "bowl of blessedness." Texans call it "a bowl of red," but no matter what it's called, chili is one of those uniquely American dishes that sparks lively debate. Nearly everyone has "the one and only recipe," but it occupies a special spot in the Southwest. Chili very likely originated in Texas, where the first nourishing pots were prepared by the chuckwagon cooks who fed cowboys on cattle drives in the mid-1850s. In fact, in 1977 the Texas legislature made it the state's official dish.

A major debate rages over whether chili should have beans in it or not. Most Texans agree on no beans so this recipe does not include them, though you could add them if you like.

The spiciness and heat of chili are largely matters of personal taste. This recipe should suit most people. Those with a preference for highly seasoned dishes may want to add more chili powder. Serve accompanied by a side dish of hot pinto beans, a stack of warm tortillas, and "fixin's" such as shredded cheese, sour cream, and minced green onions.

Heat the oil in a heavy 5-quart Dutch oven or saucepan over medium heat. Cook the beef pieces in batches, stirring often, just until the meat loses its pink color and turns gray. Set each batch aside as it is done. Add the onion and garlic to the same pan and cook over medium-high heat, stirring occasionally, for 3 to 4 minutes. Return the meat to the pan. Add the cumin, oregano, chili powder, tomatoes, chiles, and salt and cook, stirring occasionally, for 3 to 4 minutes. Add the water and bring the mixture to a boil. Lower the heat and gently simmer, uncovered, for 1 hour, stirring occasionally. The meat should be tender. If the chili seems too thick, add 1/2 cup water; if it needs thickening, add 1 tablespoon of cornmeal and heat for 5 minutes.

Yield: 8 servings

4 tablespoons unsalted butter
4 ounces (4 squares) unsweetened
    chocolate
4 large eggs, room temperature
½ teaspoon salt
1½ cups sugar
1 teaspoon vanilla
1 cup sifted all-purpose flour
1 cup coarsely chopped walnuts
    or pecans

Aunt Birdie's After-School Brownies

 These rich, chocolaty cake squares are a classic American after-school treat that taste best alongside a tall, cold glass of milk. The first brownies were probably the result of a kitchen accident. When a chocolate cake failed to rise, a smart baker refused to admit defeat and simply cut the moist, but rather flat, cake into squares.

For a quick, slightly fancier dessert, cut the brownies in larger squares than usual, top with a scoop of vanilla ice cream, plenty of hot fudge sauce, and a dollop of fresh whipped cream.

Preheat oven to 350° F.
Grease and flour a 9 x 13-inch baking pan.

In a small heavy saucepan, melt the butter and chocolate over low heat, stirring until smooth. Set aside to cool slightly.

In a medium-size mixing bowl, beat the eggs with the salt until foamy. Add the sugar and vanilla and beat until the sugar dissolves. Stir in the cooled chocolate and mix well. Fold in the flour and nuts.

Turn the batter into the baking pan and smooth the top with a spatula. Bake 20 to 25 minutes, or until a metal skewer inserted in the middle comes out with crumbs clinging to it. Be careful not to overbake. Cool and cut into 2-inch squares.

Yield: 2 dozen

1½ tablespoons active dry yeast
1 cup warm milk
1 teaspoon sugar
¼ cup sugar
½ teaspoon salt
½ cup butter, melted
About 3½ cups all-purpose flour
Melted butter for dipping

Golden State Monkey Bread

 All homemade bread is better than store-bought, but this unusual version combines home-baked goodness with a bit of whimsy. Made of buttered sections of dough baked in a circle, it rises high in the pan, forming an irregularly shaped loaf that is pulled apart rather than sliced. In California in the 1950s, it was popular to serve Monkey Bread, or Bubble Bread as it is sometimes known, at luncheons and buffets. Silly looking and silly to eat, it may have been given its whimsical moniker because the baker has to "monkey" around with the dough.

In a large bowl, sprinkle the dry yeast over the warm milk and stir in the teaspoon of sugar. Let stand for about 5 minutes, or until frothy bubbles form.

Add the sugar, salt, and melted butter to the yeast mixture and stir to combine. Add the flour ½ cup at a time, mixing well between each addition. When all of the flour has been incorporated, beat vigorously with a wooden spoon until it forms a stiff, batterlike dough (about 5 minutes). Cover the bowl with plastic wrap and set aside to rise in a warm place until doubled in size, about 1 to 1½ hours.

Punch down the dough, transfer it to a lightly floured board, and knead until the dough is smooth and satiny. Roll it out into a ½-inch rectangle and cut into diamond shapes about 2½ inches long. Dipping each diamond into melted butter, arrange the pieces in overlapping layers in a greased 9-inch ring mold or tube pan. Cover the mold with plastic wrap and set aside to rise in a warm place until almost doubled in size, about 30 minutes.

Preheat oven to 400° F.

Remove plastic wrap and bake for 30 minutes, or until golden brown. Cool for 10 minutes in the mold, then carefully turn the bread out of the mold onto a large plate.

Yield: 1 loaf

A first-rate soup is more creative than a second-rate painting.

Abraham Maslow

Native American Butternut Squash Soup

4 leeks, trimmed, washed well, and
   roughly chopped
2 tablespoons butter
1 quart water
2 cups butternut or other yellow-
   fleshed squash, cut into ½-inch
   cubes
1 cup peeled and diced celeriac
2 cloves garlic
1 cup sun-dried tomatoes
¼ cup parsley
⅓ cup brown rice
¾ cup light or heavy cream

The early American settlers were introduced by Native Americans to the countless varieties of squash that grew from one coast of America to the other. There were crooknecks in the Northeast, cushaws flourishing in the South, and acorn squash abundant in the Great Northwest. Whether roasted in their skins under a bed of campfire coals or dried in the sun for use when food supplies grew scarce in wintertime, the squashes were a sustaining, flavorful gift of nature. Today, the pear-shaped, yellow-fleshed butternut squash called for in this easy-to-make soup is one of the most popular varieties.

In a large, heavy stockpot, sauté the leeks in the butter until golden. Add the water, squash cubes, celeriac, garlic, tomatoes, and parsley and simmer until the vegetables are tender, about 45 minutes.

Remove the solid ingredients from the pot with a slotted spoon. Using a food processor with a metal blade or a food mill, purée the solids and set them aside.

Add the rice to the liquid remaining in the pot and simmer until cooked, about 1 hour.

Return the puréed ingredients to the pot, add the cream, and heat gently at a simmer before serving. If you prefer a thinner consistency, add a little water.

Yield: 4 to 6 servings

Johnny Appleseed Cider Wassail

3 cinnamon sticks
2 bay leaves
1 teaspoon whole cloves
1 teaspoon whole allspice
2 star anise pods
12½ cups cider
1¼ cups brandy
¼ cup Calvados
¼ cup honey
Whole cloves for garnish
3 small firm eating apples,
    peeled, cored, and cut into sixths

Warm cider-based drinks have long been a welcome feature at wintertime family gatherings. Whether it's a steaming punch cup filled with this spicy wassail to ring in the winter holidays and spread good cheer or a simple steaming mug of cinnamon-scented mulled cider to warm the hands and heart after a few spins around the skating ring or frozen pond, there is succor in cider when the cold winds of winter blow strongest.

Nearly all early American cookbooks included instructions on how to concoct a wide variety of cider-based beverages with colorful names such as Artillery Punch, Spinster's Night Cap, Temperance Punch, and Sleeper's Cider.

Tie the cinnamon sticks, bay leaves, 1 teaspoon of the whole cloves, the allspice, and star anise pods together in a square of cheesecloth to form a spice bag. Set aside.

In a large pot, combine the cider, brandy, and Calvados. Gently bring to a boil. Add the spice bag and the honey. Stir well. Reduce the heat and simmer gently for 10 minutes.

Stick several cloves in each apple slice and add the apples to the wassail. Simmer for 3 minutes. Remove the spice bag.

To serve, pour the wassail into a punch bowl and garnish with the apples. The wassail is equally nice served hot or warm.

Yield: about 13 cups

For the cheddar crust:
2 cups all-purpose flour
1/2 teaspoon salt
1 cup chilled vegetable shortening
3/4 cup grated cheddar cheese
1/2 cup ice water

For the apple-cheddar filling:
2 tablespoons all-purpose flour
3/4 teaspoon ground cinnamon
1/4 teaspoon ground nutmeg
2 1/2 pounds cooking apples,
*   peeled, cored, and sliced*
3/4 cup light brown sugar
1 teaspoon fresh lemon juice
1 teaspoon finely cut lemon zest
2 tablespoons unsalted butter, cut in
*   bits*
1/4 cup grated cheddar cheese

County Fair Apple-Cheddar Pie

Long before Johnny Appleseed, whose real name was John Chapman, planted his historic apple seedlings, early colonists kept their homes in "apple pie order" and ate apple pie for breakfast. Each household had a cherished recipe and many a young bride's dowry included a barrelful of dried apples to see her through her first winter's baking. Nineteenth-century cooks set steaming, fresh-baked pies to cool on the window sill or tucked them away in "pie safes," elevated wooden cabinets with punched tin fronts that were kept out on the enclosed back porch. There were literally hundreds of varieties of apples to choose from, with delightful names such as Pink Pearl, Maiden Blush, Roxbury Russet, and Westfield Seek-No-Further.

Today's blue-ribbon bakers believe Northern Spys make the best pies because the juicy, sweetly tart slices stay nice and firm during baking. Other good choices include Granny Smiths, Jonathans, and Macouns.

In a large bowl, combine the flour and salt. Using your fingertips or a pastry blender, cut the shortening and cheese into the flour until it resembles coarse meal. Sprinkle 1 tablespoon of ice water at a time over the mixture, quickly mixing with a fork after each addition (use only enough water for the dough to hold together). Form dough into a ball, cut in half, flatten slightly into disks, and wrap individually in plastic wrap. Chill for 30 minutes.

Preheat oven to 450° F.

In a large bowl, combine all of the filling ingredients except the cheese and toss to coat.

On a lightly floured surface, roll out disk of dough into a 10-inch circle. Transfer the pastry to a 9-inch deep-dish pie pan, gently pressing it into place.

Mound the apple filling in the pie shell and sprinkle the cheese over the top. Roll out the second disk of dough. Place the pastry on top of the filling and crimp the edges together. Cut slits in the top. Bake for 10 minutes, reduce temperature to 350° F, and continue baking for 30 minutes, or until the crust is golden. Serve warm or at room temperature.

Yield: 6 to 8 servings

Spicebox Gingerbread

2 cups sifted all-purpose flour
½ teaspoon salt
1 teaspoon ground ginger
1 teaspoon baking soda
8 tablespoons unsalted butter
½ cup firmly packed brown sugar
2 large eggs, room temperature,
    separated
½ cup sour cream
½ cup unsulphured molasses

There's history in each fragrant morsel of this gingerbread and we owe it all to Amelia Simmons, who wrote a little book called *American Cookery* in 1796, just 20 years after the Declaration of Independence was signed. Back when home cooks wrote their favorite recipes by hand in dogeared "receipt" books and kept their precious spices in a tin spicebox in the pantry, Amelia's book was the first to gather together basic recipes and acknowledge the flavors and ingredients unique to American cookery. It included the first known recipe for a soft-textured gingerbread made with molasses, the most commonly used sweetener in the days when sugar was scarce and costly.

This version honors the past but includes sour cream for added moistness and soft texture. Hinting at the goodness to come, the cozy, spice-scented aroma while it's baking will perfume the whole house. Serve warm or at room temperature, topped with whipped cream or vanilla ice cream. And remember Amelia Simmons, the "mother of American cookbooks."

Preheat oven to 350° F.
Grease and flour a 9 x 5 x 3-inch loaf pan. Sift together the flour, salt, ginger, and baking soda and set aside.

In a large mixing bowl, cream the butter until soft and slightly fluffy. Add the sugar a little at a time, beating until smooth. Beat the egg yolks well and add to the butter-sugar mixture. Combine the sour cream and molasses and add to the mixture, alternating with the flour.

Beat the egg whites until stiff and fold them into the batter. Spoon the batter into the prepared pan, gently pushing the mixture into the corners.

Bake 50 to 60 minutes, or until a metal skewer inserted in the middle comes out clean and dry.

Yield: 1 loaf

Succulent Salmon with Capers

4 salmon steaks or fillets,
   about 12 ounces each and
   ¾-inch thick
2 tablespoons unsalted butter or
   corn oil
¼ teaspoon salt
¼ teaspoon freshly ground
   black pepper
4 tablespoons chopped fresh chives
2 tablespoons capers, drained
4 thin slices of lemon
6 tablespoons dry white wine or fresh
   lemon juice

 The Native Americans of the Pacific Northwest had more than 50 ways of serving salmon, and in many Native American languages the words for salmon and for fish were the same. The fish was eaten fresh or dried and smoked. Most delicious of all was "planked" salmon, made by skewering fresh fish onto a piece of driftwood which was set over the embers of a fire to cook. On the East Coast in Colonial days, salmon were so cheap and plentiful that some servants actually stipulated in their working agreements that they could not be fed salmon more than once a week. Today, salmon is a relatively expensive delicacy that tastes best when cooked rather simply. The capers in this recipe provide a hint of extra flavor, and their green color enhances the rosy hues of the salmon.

Preheat oven to 350° F.

Arrange the fish in a single layer in a large, shallow baking dish. Place ½ tablespoon of butter on top of each piece.

Season with salt and pepper and sprinkle with the chopped chives and capers. Top each piece with a lemon slice.

Sprinkle the wine or lemon juice over the fish. Bake for 20 minutes.

Yield: 4 servings

List of Plates

Index